Index Card

Games

for

ESL

Revised Edition

Supplementary Materials Handbook One

Compiled by
Staff, English Language Department
The School for International Training:
Ruthanne Brown, Marilyn Bean Barrett, Joseph Bennett, Robert Carvutto, Janet Gaston,
Harlan Harris, Bonnie Mennell, Oden Oak, Phillip Stantial, Elizabeth Tannenbaum, and
Susan Treadgold. Illustrated by Patrick R. Moran.

Revised and edited by

Raymond C. Clark

PRO LINGUA ASSOCIATES

Publishers

Published by Pro Lingua Associates
15 Elm Street
Brattleboro, Vermont 05301
800-366-4775
SAN 216-0579

ISBN 0-86647-052-2

Library of Congress Cataloguing in Publication Data

    Main entry under title:
    Index card games for ESL.
      (Supplementary materials handbook ; 1)
    students. 2 Educational Games. I. Brown, Ruthanne.
    II. Clark, Raymond C., 1937–   . III. Title: Index
    card games for E.S.L. IV. Series.
    PE1128.A2I47 1982   428'.007'1073   82-9786
                                        AACR2

Designed by Arthur A. Burrows
Printed in the United States of America

Second edition. Fifth printing 1998
15,000 copies in print

128
ND
=1

Acknowledgements

This collection of card games is the work of many hands — most belonging to former members of the English Department staff at The School for International Training. As the reviser and editor of the card games, I have tried to find out just whose hands did play an important part in the development of the concept and the preliminary version of the book. To the best of my knowledge, the following people played key roles in developing the games: Ruthanne Brown, who got things started, Marilyn Bean Barrett, Joe Bennett, Robert Carvutto, Jan Gaston, Harland Harris, Bonnie Mennell, Oden Oak, Phil Stantial, Elizabeth Tannenbaum and Susan Treadgold. Three other members of the English department also offered support and encouragement: Karen Kale, Bobbi Williams and Emmett McKowen.

I would also like to acknowledge the cooperation of Alvino Fantini who, as the director of The Experiment Press, granted permission to Pro Lingua Associates to publish the first revision of the original games.

Thanks are also due to the following people who contributed to the development and production of the first printing: Pat Moran for his illustrations, Susan McBean for typing the manuscript, Lisa Cook for setting the text type, and Andy Burrows for his assistance in the design of the book.

Finally, let me say that although this present edition is only possible because of the work of the original contributors mentioned above, I have made many changes in the original version and a few more in this third, updated printing, and I sincerely hope that I have enhanced their ideas. If I have not, I hope they will forgive me.

RCC

Table of Contents

Introduction

This book is the starting point for what could be an extensive collection of Index Card Games for you or your department. We have provided simple directions for six kinds of games and a number of suggestions for specific games of each type. As a starting point, try some of the specific games we have suggested and then once you get the hang of it, you will undoubtedly want to add games of your own to your collection. You will need to invest in a supply of 3 x 5 index cards to make your games, but by following our suggestions they won't take long to make, and once made they can be used over and over.

The games can be one of the most enjoyable supplementary activities you can do with your class whether you use them once a week or once a day. In an intensive language program you can easily use one a day and the students will not tire of them because they provide a pleasant and relaxing break from the hard work of battling with a stubborn language. Because the games are by nature a supplementary activity and a time-out from the rigors of formal teaching and learning, they are best used to review or practice words and sentences that have already been introduced. In a limited way however, the games can be used to introduce new bits and pieces of language -- especially vocabulary items and idioms.

Beyond the fact that the games are fun and a welcome change of pace, they are also useful. As mentioned above, they can serve as a painless review of previously studied material. They are also invaluable in helping build the class into a cohesive group, as long as the competitive aspect of the games is not taken seriously. In several of the games, groups of students have to work together toward a common goal -- whether it be solving a problem or building up points and trying to win. In the process of working together, the students necessarily have to interact with each other to help, support, suggest, encourage, correct and even challenge each other.

1

Inevitably, some teasing, joking, cheering, and playful booing pervade the classroom. In short, the games give everyone, teacher included, a chance to play and be playful. In a language classroom, play is useful.

These language games are useful in one other important way -- they remove you the teacher from the spotlight and allow the students to deal with each other and the cards in front of them. You are there, of course. You get things started and total up the score and serve as the impartial referee, but you can stay out of the way for a while and let the players play.

Throughout the book we have graded our suggestions as being suitable for elementary, intermediate or advanced classes. Please accept these labels with the understanding that they are not rigid. The more important point is that the games can be enjoyed by students at all levels. After some experience you will develop a good sense for what your class can do and can't do.

Have fun!

Matched Pairs

BRIEF DESCRIPTION:

Similar to the TV show <u>Concentration</u>, these games require the students to remember the location of the cards and to make pairs.

PURPOSE:

To review vocabulary. Sometimes, new words can be added to the set, as long as the number of new words is small and not disruptive. A second purpose, if the game is played as a team activity, is to stimulate conversation among the team members -- "I think seven matches twenty-three". "Do you remember where _____ is?" Finally, the game, like all the card games, is fun and contributes to group building.

PREPARATION:

Choose a category, e.g. antonyms. Write a word on each of 15 cards and the matching antonym on another 15 cards. Shuffle the cards well and then turn them over and number them from 1 to 30 on the back.

Because the purpose of this game is to review something that has been taught rather than teach something new, go over the pairs before the game begins to be sure everybody knows what the 15 pairs are.

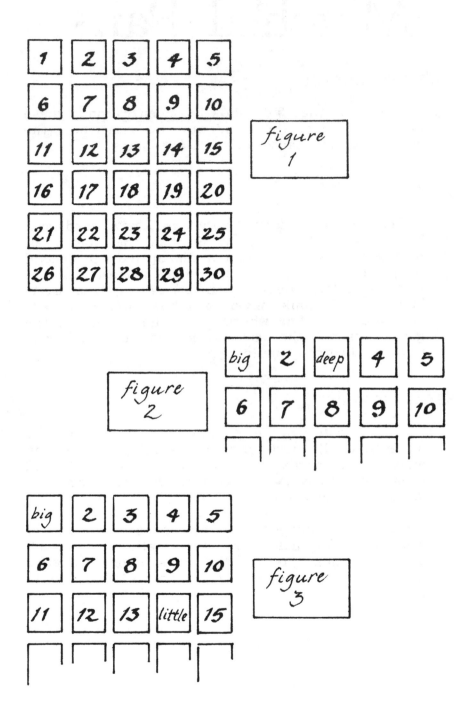

1	2	3	4	5
6	7	8	9	10
11	12	13	14	15
16	17	18	19	20
21	22	23	24	25
26	27	28	29	30

figure
1

figure
2

big	2	deep	4	5
6	7	8	9	10

big	2	3	4	5
6	7	8	9	10
11	12	13	little	15

figure
3

PROCEDURE:

1. Lay the cards out face down with the numbers showing, as in Figure 1.

2. Taking turns, the students call out two numbers, e.g. 1 and 3. Turn over the called cards. If the cards don't match (chances are they won't for the first few turns) the cards are turned back over. In figure 2, we see that big and deep don't match so they are turned face down again.

3. When a student makes a match (figure 3) he removes the matched cards from the lay-out and gets another turn. He continues until he fails to produce a match.

4. When all the cards have been matched, the student with the largest pile wins.

VARIATIONS:

1. The game can be played as a team activity. One person from each team is the spokesperson for the team's collective effort to remember locations. Students can take turns being the spokesperson.

2. When a match is made, the player can be required to use the two words in a sentence. If the player fails the cards are returned to the lay-out, and the next player gets the opportunity to match and use the two words.

SUGGESTIONS:

1. Synonyms*

2. Antonyms*

3. Two-word verbs*

4. Homonyms

5. Like vowel sounds

6. Like beginning or ending sounds

7. Proverbs*

8. Idioms*

9. Countries and their corresponding languages

10. Prefixes and base words*

11. Verb forms -- simple/past; past/past participle

12. Pictures of objects and their corresponding word*

13. Comparatives

14. Vocabulary selected from readings -- words and definitions or synonyms.

* See sample games detailed on the following pages.

Adjective Synonyms

big	large
near	close
sick	ill
simple	easy
little	small
quick	fast
right	correct
difficult	hard
certain	sure
tall	high
many	a lot of .
cheap	inexpensive
far	distant
happy	glad
angry	mad

Adjective Synonyms

next	following
shy	timid
afraid	scared
huge	very large
slender	thin
good-looking	attractive
well-known	famous
wealthy	rich
dull	boring
lucky	fortunate
intelligent	smart
amusing	funny
enough	sufficient
terrible	awful
total	complete

Adjective Synonyms

skeptical	doubtful
eccentric	strange
shocking	surprising
troubled	worried
courageous	brave
bright	smart
selfish	egotistical
nervous	anxious
calm	peaceful
candid	frank
truthful	honest
uneasy	apprehensive
jealous	envious
careful	cautious
precise	exact

Adjective Antonyms

short	long
old	new
little	big
fat	thin
cold	hot
wet	dry
high	low
tall	short
warm	cool
good	bad
old	young
happy	sad
far	near
cheap	expensive
wide	narrow

Adjective Antonyms

single	married
polite	rude
easy	hard
soft	hard
full	hungry
full	empty
light	dark
light	heavy
drunk	sober
clean	dirty
dead	alive
handsome	ugly
strong	weak
bright	dull
sharp	dull

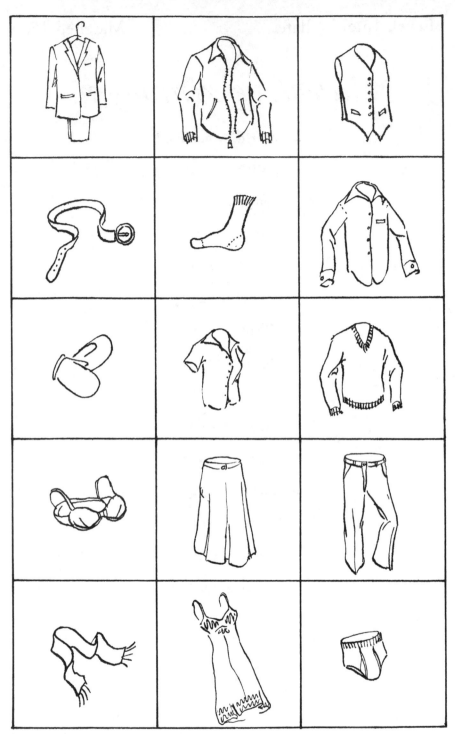

The illustrations above are matched with words on the next page. Permission is hereby given to copy the pictures for mounting on cards.

Clothing

suit

jacket

vest

belt

sock

shirt

mittens

blouse

sweater

bra

skirt

pants

scarf

slip

underpants

Two-word Verbs
(separable)

call up	telephone
call back	telephone again
pick out	choose
put on	dress
give back	return
take off	remove
talk over	discuss
do over	repeat
fill out	complete
find out	discover
turn on	activate
look over	examine
leave out	omit
call off	cancel
put back	replace

Two-word Verbs
(inseparable)

come back	return
call on	visit
look after	take care of
look like	resemble
get over	recover
wait on	serve
run into	meet by chance
run out of	consume completely
pick on	bother
run over	hit by a car
keep on	continue
go over	review
look into	investigate
get along with	be friendly with
look for	search

15

Two-word Verbs
(all types)

show up	appear
take up	begin to study
drop off	leave
make up	invent
put out	extinguish
pass out	distribute
pass out	faint
bring up	raise
turn down	reduce the volume
figure out	solve
put off	postpone
turn in	retire
talk back to	answer rudely
look up to	respect
throw away	discard

Synonyms
(human qualities and stages)

courteous	polite
infant	baby
shy	bashful
beautiful	lovely
rude	impolite
humorous	funny
adolescent	juvenile
courageous	brave
smart	intelligent
square	conventional
stupid	foolish
immature	childish
diligent	hard-working
conceited	stuck up
up-tight	anxious

Note: Unlike the previous lists, this has a semantic rather than a grammatical theme. For lists of some other semantic categories, see The ESL Miscellany, Resource Handbook Number Two, Pro Lingua Associates, Brattleboro, Vermont.

17

Prefixes

mis	understand
dis	agree
un	believable
un	attractive
un	pleasant
im	polite
dis	satisfied
un	fortunate
in	dependent
un	happy
un	button
mis	pronounce
dis	approve
in	correct
dis	obey

18

Idioms

on purpose	intentionally
as a rule	usually
on hand	available
so far	until now
in fact	really
so long	goodbye
never mind	don't worry
by all means	certainly
from now on	from this moment forward
no wonder	it isn't surprising
right away	immediately
for good	permanently
by the way	incidentally
out of order	not working
off and on	irregularly, occasionally

Proverbs

People who live in glass houses	shouldn't throw stones.
Don't cry	over spilled milk.
All that glitters	is not gold.
He who hesitates	is lost.
Where there's a will	there's a way.
Still waters	run deep.
Don't judge a book	by its cover.
When the cat's away	the mice will play.
Too many cooks	spoil the broth.
A stitch in time	saves nine.
He who laughs last	laughs best.
Laughter	is the best medicine.
Time	heals all things.
Better late	than never.
Easier said	than done.

Sound and Spell

BRIEF DESCRIPTION:

Each card has one word written on it and one sound underlined, e.g. br<u>ie</u>f. A set of cards (30 is a good number) contains from 2 to 6 different sounds. The cards are shuffled and given to the students who sort them into separate piles, one pile for each different sound.

PURPOSE:

The students review the pronunciation of selected sounds and the various ways the sounds can be spelled.

PREPARATION:

Select sounds that the students need to practice, e.g. /iy/ and /i/, and write a number of words, each containing the same sound, on a number of cards -- one to a card. Underline the spelling of the sound in question. Select a variety of troublesome spellings. For example:

gr<u>ee</u>n	f<u>ie</u>ld	n<u>ea</u>t
pol<u>i</u>ce	p<u>eo</u>ple	sk<u>i</u>

A duplicate set should be prepared for each group of students; in general, students can do this game with 3-5 people per group.

Then assemble a set of cards containing at least two different sounds. In other words, a set of 30 cards could contain 15 examples of /iy/ and 15 examples of /i/. A suggested combination for an interesting game is 5 sounds, each represented by 6 different words.

PROCEDURE:

1. Give the directions to the class, e.g. "You have 30 cards in this set. There are 5 different sounds and 6 cards for each sound. Work together. Read the words, pronounce them and sort them into 5 piles. When you have them all sorted, I will check them."

2. Allow the students to work on the sounds. Do not give any help.

3. When all groups have finished their sorting, have the groups lay out their cards and look at each other's solutions.

4. Check over the solutions and announce the winner(s) -- the team with the most correct cards.

VARIATIONS:

1. To make the game more challenging, put a "wild card" in each group -- one sound that is completely different from the others.

2. Use sets with uneven numbers of cards, e.g. five /iy/; four /i/; seven /ay/; eight /ey/ and six /e/.

3. Establish a time limit to the game. A three minute egg timer can be a useful gadget for this and other timed activities.

4. When all teams have finished and a winner has been declared, review the cards aloud as a group.

SUGGESTIONS:

1. vowels and diphthongs*

2. consonants*

3. consonant clusters

4. silent letters

5. homonyms

6. minimal pairs

7. stress patterns, e.g. words with stress on 1st syllable, 2nd syllable, 3rd syllable, etc.

* See sample games on the following pages.

/i/	/iy/	/ay/
sit	green	like
this	teeth	wide
miss	three	life
think	seat	my
mister	please	try
still	neat	sky
tip	these	type
give	here[+]	right
office	near[+]	knife
physical	zero[+]	climate
typical	sheet	tiny
build	steal	sign
rich	people	island
pretty	police	lie
busy	ski	height
English	ceiling	guy
been	field	size
women	heal	fight

* Within each column the spellings begin with easy, regular patterns and end with more unusual spellings.

[+] Sometimes pronounced /i/.

/e/	/ey/	/æ/
red	place	man
left	waste	ran
met	ate	add
fell	same	glad
dead	ache	dad
bread	tape	sad
weather	plain	plan
heavy	straight	flat
any	rain	have
many	eight	glad
led	weight	cash
ready	neighbor	back
meant	play	campus
said	way	ashtray
says	patient	napkin
friend	razor	planned
guess	great	happy
end	cafe	shall

/a/*	/ɔ/*	/ə/
n<u>o</u>t	c<u>o</u>st	s<u>o</u>n
c<u>o</u>t	<u>o</u>ff	t<u>o</u>n
g<u>o</u>t	<u>o</u>f·ten	s<u>o</u>me
st<u>o</u>p	b<u>o</u>ss	m<u>o</u>nth
sh<u>o</u>t	<u>a</u>ll	n<u>o</u>ne
b<u>o</u>x	c<u>a</u>ll	l<u>o</u>ve
J<u>o</u>hn	l<u>aw</u>	c<u>u</u>p
bl<u>o</u>ck	<u>aw</u>ful	b<u>u</u>t
h<u>o</u>bby	c<u>au</u>se	l<u>u</u>ck
cl<u>o</u>ck	f<u>au</u>lt	s<u>u</u>ng
kn<u>o</u>b	p<u>au</u>se	wh<u>a</u>t
b<u>o</u>mb	d<u>au</u>ghter	w<u>a</u>s
h<u>o</u>nor	th<u>ou</u>ght	d<u>oe</u>s
c<u>o</u>mma	c<u>o</u>ugh	y<u>ou</u>ng
st<u>ar</u>	<u>ou</u>ght	r<u>ou</u>gh
<u>a</u>re	dr<u>aw</u>	bl<u>oo</u>d
f<u>a</u>ther	c<u>au</u>ght	c<u>ou</u>ntry
h<u>ea</u>rt	t<u>a</u>ll	<u>o</u>nion

* Many native speakers distinguish these sounds in different ways or do not make a distinction. Check your own pronunciation of these sounds before you make up a set of cards.

/aw/	/ow/	/oy/
town	cold	joy
crowd	both	boy
vowel	wrote	toy
allow	stove	point
drown	no	coin
flower	more	voice
sound	coat	destroy
loud	soap	employ
our	toast	annoy
ounce	loaf	poison
count	blow	toilet
shout	throw	moist
flour	folk	voyage
couch	plateau	enjoy
towel	owe	Detroit
house	Joe	avoid
cow	grow	invoice
doubt	though	oil

27

/u/	/uw/	/yuw/
put	do	music
pull	to	cute
push	who	future
good	choose	cube
look	food	use
wood	you	usual
cook	spoon	humid
stood	lose	Utah
would	fruit	few
should	suit	cue
full	tube	menu
foot	new	huge
cookie	loose	community
woman	soup	beauty
could	through	museum
bull	glue	view
brook	shoe	pure

/ər/	/s/	/z/
her	some	zoo
were	books	zero
player	city	lazy
third	ask	zebra
dirt	this	easy
shirt	pencil	these
person	simple	zipper
hurt	sentence	please
burn	pass	trees
turn	accept	is
first	acid	rise
purse	loose	lose
word	psychology	Zimbabwe
worst	science	he's
church	sword	jazz
pearl	ceiling	was
heard	jumps	xerox
thirteen	listen	Xavier

/k/	/č/	/š/
keep	child	shoe
kind	chair	ship
back	inch	she
neck	each	wash
car	watch	fish
make	catch	cash
king	reach	show
college	which	sure
public	cheese	sugar
break	rich	wish
check	witch	special
ache	much	Chicago
Christ	cheap	ocean
chorus	cello	action
success	concerto	motion
school	actual	chef
rock	wrench	chauffeur
liquor	itch	sheep

Scrambled Sentences

BRIEF DESCRIPTION:

The students re-arrange jumbled sentences, e.g.

the | ? | go | they | downtown | in | Do | afternoon

Each word and punctuation mark is written on a separate card.

PURPOSE:

This game is useful for reviewing word order and the placement of punctuation marks.

PREPARATION:

The game is more effective if it concentrates on a single sentence pattern, e.g. questions in the simple present tense. Write out a sentence with each word and punctuation mark on a separate card. In general, it is best to capitalize the first word in the sentence.

Do | they | go | downtown | in | the | afternoon | ?

To keep the various sentences from becoming mixed up, it is useful to write a number on each card, e.g.

5-10 sentences will be sufficient for an interesting game.

Shuffle the cards in each sentence and put a rubber band around each sentence.

Finally, make a list of all sentences for your own reference and for use in Step #5 below.

PROCEDURE:

1. Divide the class into groups of 2-3 students.

2. Give each group a sentence and put the extras in the middle of the room.

3. Tell each group that it must use all the cards to form a sentence.

4. When a group is satisfied with its sentence, it writes the number of the sentence and the sentence on a separate sheet of paper. Then the group returns its sentence to the middle and chooses a new bundle of cards.

5. When the groups have finished, read the correct sentences and have the groups check their answers.

VARIATIONS:

1. Have the groups read their answer sheets to each other.

2. The first group to finish can write its answers on the board.

3. Instead of working at the sentence level, the students can try working at the paragraph level, arranging sentences into coherent paragraphs.

4. The numbered sentences can also be arranged into a paragraph.

5. To make the game more challenging and to allow for more variations, do not capitalize the first letter of the first word in the sentence.

SUGGESTIONS:

1. verb tenses*

2. question formation*

3. conditional forms*

4. modal auxiliaries

5. passive voice

6. tag questions

7. prepositions

8. gerunds and infinitives

9. causative

10. imbedded questions and statements

11. indirect speech

12. relative clauses*

13. clauses with when and while*

14. conjunctions

15. adjective order

16. comparatives*

17. superlatives

18. scrambled paragraphs*

19. sentences and paragraphs taken from readings done in class

* see sample games on the following pages.

Simple Present

1. I receive a letter from my family once a week.
2. He eats breakfast at 7:30 every morning.
3. She likes tomato juice and orange juice, but she doesn't like grapefruit juice.
4. He doesn't like the food in the cafeteria.
5. Do you go to the movies every Saturday?
6. What do you usually do on Sunday afternoons in your country?
7. What time do you get up every morning?
8. Where are you from?
9. Excuse me. Is this your pen?
10. Do you live in a dormitory or in an apartment?

Past

1. They went there by plane.
2. We didn't see them at the disco last weekend.
3. How many students were absent yesterday?
4. I didn't do my homework last night because I was sick.
5. He bought a new shirt yesterday and wore it to class this morning.
6. Did they go to the party together or alone?
7. I didn't go to the meeting yesterday, but Joe did.
8. I saw a good movie at the theater next to the bank last night.
9. When did he mail the letter to his girlfriend?
10. He called his father in Venezuela Tuesday night after dinner.

35

Questions

1. How far is your apartment from here?

2. Where did you live last year?

3. Who called last night?

4. Do you like cream in your coffee?

5. Did you visit your friend in Turkey when you traveled in the Middle East?

6. What will you do after you finish your English course?

7. How many Big Macs would you like?

8. Where were you born?

9. What time are you going to get up in the morning?

10. Why did Susan go downtown after school yesterday?

Comparatives

1. Carlos is taller than José but shorter than Ali.

2. Is your teacher more handsome than Paul Newman?

3. Her hair is longer than yours.

4. Is the Amazon River wider than the Mississippi?

5. Chinese is as difficult as English.

6. Discotheques are more exciting in Brazil than in the United States.

7. The weather is worse than it was this morning.

8. It isn't raining as hard as it was.

9. Is it farther from New York to Chicago than from New York to Washington, D.C.?

10. German beer is better than American beer.

Present Perfect

1. He has gotten his passport, but he has not received his I-20 yet.

2. Have you ever met the man who works in the drugstore downtown?

3. How long have they lived in your town?

4. He hasn't had time to do his homework yet.

5. I have not been to New York since I arrived in the United States three months ago.

6. My friend has never been to Chicago, but she has been to San Francisco.

7. Bill has lived in the same house since he was born.

8. I have studied English for five years.

9. She has talked to her mother every night this week.

10. He has just returned from a vacation in Mexico.

Relative Clauses

1. Those boys with whom he spoke yesterday are studying English with me.

2. The lesson which we did yesterday was very difficult.

3. I finally met the woman who lives in the apartment next to mine.

4. Did you buy the shirt that we saw in the store window yesterday?

5. He doesn't know any of the people who work in the Spanish Department.

6. John Stewart, whose brother just called, will be back in the dorm at five o'clock.

7. Is this the book that you wanted me to return to the library for you?

8. The girl whose luggage was lost is from Mexico.

9. The police caught the man who stole your purse.

10. I gave the telegram which just arrived to your brother.

Past Perfect

1. Susan had spoken with her brother ten minutes before he had the accident.

2. They had been waiting for two hours when the train finally arrived.

3. I had lived in the U.S. for three months before I was able to speak English.

4. Her friends had just finished dinner when she arrived.

5. The police arrested the man after he had stolen the car.

6. Had you ever studied English before you came to the United States?

7. After he had been in Boston for two weeks, he found a job which paid very well.

8. They had just left for the movies when we arrived at their house.

9. What had you studied in your country before you came to the United States?

10. He had never studied the conditional until he took an English class at the University.

Clauses with
When and While

1. They had an accident while they were driving to Miami.

2. What were you doing yesterday when I called?

3. The fire began while we were studying in the library.

4. We had a flat tire while we were crossing the bridge.

5. I was feeling better when the doctor arrived.

6. The wind was blowing hard when Susan got up this morning.

7. We got married while she was living in Massachusetts.

8. We were playing football while Jim was mowing the lawn.

9. Someone stole her purse while she was shopping downtown.

10. I was dancing at the disco while you were studying in your room.

Conditionals

1. I would not have been so angry yesterday if you had told me the truth.

2. He would not have so many accidents if he were a better driver.

3. We will go home early from school if it snows.

4. If it were not so late, I would invite you to my house for a drink.

5. If I had paid attention in class, I would have passed the English test.

6. If the doctor calls, please take his number and tell him that I will call him back this afternoon.

7. I would have visited you in San Francisco last winter if I had had more time.

8. If I were President of the United States, I would live on Pennsylvania Avenue in Washington, D.C.

9. If you get a promotion, will you have to travel overseas for your company?

10. If I had invited you to my house yesterday, would you have come?

Conjunctive Adverbs

1. I was given a free ticket to the concert; otherwise, I would not have gone.

2. They do not like cold weather; consequently, they are going to go to Florida for the winter.

3. His mother does not like pets; therefore, she will not let him have a dog.

4. Nobody knew the meaning of the word; furthermore, we could not find it in the dictionary.

5. Jack never studies; in addition, he always comes to class late.

6. I went to Bob's party last night; however, I wish I hadn't.

7. She had never skied before; nevertheless, she came down the mountain easily.

8. I prefer to use cash when I shop; however, my husband prefers to use credit cards.

9. I would like to change my doctor's appointment to Tuesday; otherwise, I will not be able to see him this week.

10. He does not speak English very well; therefore, he will need to study it for another semester before he enters the University.

Operation

1. First, put the cassette into the player.
2. Then plug the microphone jack into the player.
3. Be sure the microphone is off.
4. Push both the play and record buttons.
5. To record, push the switch on the microphone.
6. To stop, push the switch off.
7. To listen, first push stop.
8. Then push rewind.
9. Finally, push play and listen.

Time Sequence

1. Bob left his house at 7:30 this morning.
2. He took his car to the train station and parked it there.
3. Then he got on the train and rode for one hour to the city.
4. When he arrived in the city, he got off the train and walked six blocks to his office.
5. He arrived at 8:55.
6. At 9:00 he sat down at his desk and began to work.

Story

1. One day a large truck filled with one hundred penguins broke down on the highway outside of a large city.

2. The driver of the truck was trying to decide what to do when a man driving a big, empty bus stopped and offered to help.

3. The truck driver said, "I have to take these penguins to the zoo right away. If you will take them in your bus, I will give you two hundred dollars."

4. The bus driver agreed to take them.

5. He put all the penguins into his bus and drove away.

6. Later that afternoon, after he had repaired the truck, the truck driver was driving through the city when he saw the bus driver with the hundred penguins.

7. He was walking along the sidewalk followed by the penguins walking two by two in a line.

8. The truck driver stopped immediately.

9. He got out of his truck and said to the bus driver, "I told you to take these penguins to the zoo!"

10. "I did," replied the bus driver, "but I had some money left over, so now I'm taking them to the movies."

Story

1. One day a clever man named Hiroshi went to a restaurant and ordered Japanese noodles.

2. After he had eaten, he asked for his check which came to sixteen sen.

3. He decided that he did not want to pay this amount.

4. He took out his wallet and counted out the money into the waiter's hand.

5. "One, two, three, four, five, six, seven, eight . . . ," he said.

6. He paused and asked the waiter what time it was.

7. "Nine," replied the waiter.

8. "Ten, eleven, twelve, thirteen, fourteen, fifteen, sixteen," continued Hiroshi.

9. The waiter didn't notice that he had been cheated out of one sen.

10. Another man who was sitting in the restaurant observed what had happened.

11. He thought this was a good trick and decided to try it.

12. The next afternoon he returned to the restaurant and ordered Japanese noodles.

13. When it came time to pay, he started counting the money into the waiter's hand, just as Hiroshi had done.

14. "One, two, three, four, five, six, seven, eight . . . ," he said.

15. Then he paused, just as Hiroshi had done, and asked the waiter what time it was.

16. "Four," the waiter replied.

17. With that, the man resumed counting, "Five, six, seven, eight, nine, ten, eleven, twelve, thirteen, fourteen, fifteen, sixteen."

45

Categories

BRIEF DESCRIPTION:

Students are given several words all belonging to one category. For example, "things that are red." While one student gives clues, his teammates guess the words belonging to the category. This game is similar to the TV show The $10,000 Pyramid.

PURPOSE:

This game requires the students to use English quickly and descriptively. It's a good exercise to "stretch" the students' command of the language.

PREPARATION:

Write two to six words on a card with the category at the top of the card. Easier ones are "colors," "adjectives of size," "things in a classroom." More difficult categories are "things you put air into," "things that a doctor uses," etc. Easy categories can be made more difficult by putting in one difficult word.

PROCEDURE:

1. Divide the class into two or more teams.

2. Give a card to a team member from one team. Leave the room with the team member to be sure he understands the meanings of the words on his card.

3. The team member announces the category to his team and then gives clues while the team tries to guess the words in the category. For example, the person with the card might say "The category is things that are hot." "It is in the sky and gives us heat and light." And the team answers with "the sun." Gestures cannot be used.

4. The team gets one point for each correct answer.

5. When the first team is finished, the next team gets a chance with a different card.

6. Four or five rounds is enough for a good game.

VARIATIONS:

1. The game can be timed -- 15 seconds to one minute to complete the list, depending on the level of the students.

2. The teams that are waiting can be shown the card to increase their interest as the guessing team tries to get the words.

3. It does not have to be done as a team activity. The entire class can be the team as one student presents the category and clues.

4. Using a stop watch, determine the winner by the total amount of time taken to do all the cards --with a maximum of one minute per card. Therefore, if each team did six cards and Team A required four minutes and Team B did all six cards in three minutes, fifty seconds, Team B wins, regardless of the number of correct guesses.

SUGGESTIONS:

1. Things that are (colors) red, green*, blue, etc.
2. Things that are (sizes) large*, small, wide, short, long, narrow, long and narrow*, etc.
3. Things that are typically (nationality) American*, Mexican, Italian, Chinese, etc.
4. Things that are found in a (place) classroom*, hotel, park, university*, city, state*, country, jewelry store*, factory, sea, kitchen*, etc.
5. Things that are (adjective) funny, easy, round*, striped, soft, old, hot*, expensive, cold, etc.

6. Things that a (profession) teacher, doctor, carpenter*, farmer, housewife, etc. needs/uses.

7. Words that are (parts of speech) nouns, verbs, adjectives*, adverbs, two-word verbs*, etc.

8. Things you need to travel*, study, drive, etc.

9. Things with a hole*, motor, light, hair, etc.

10. Things you travel in/on*.

11. Words that begin with the letter a, b, c, etc.*

12. Words that end with the letter a, b, c, etc.*

13. Words that begin/end with th, ph, st, etc.

14. Things to play*, read, study, watch, listen to*, ride, etc.

15. Things that are part of summer, fall, winter*, spring.

16. Things above*, below, around you.

17. Things used by a woman, man, child*, etc.

18. Things that are eaten, driven, opened*, cut, read, worn, filled, etc.

19. Things you do with your body, feet*, etc.

20. Familiar quotes, expressions, slang, etc.

21. Names of professions*, countries, languages, cities, clothing*, parts of the body*, fruit, vegetables*, food*, famous people, furniture*, animals*, electrical appliances*, relatives*, stores*, parts of a car, sports*, etc.

For more ideas and lists for topical and cultural categories, see The ESL Miscellany, Resource Handbook Number Two, Pro Lingua Associates, Brattleboro, Vermont.

*See sample games on the following pages.

Things that are green

grass
lettuce
peppers
trees
peas
dollar

Things that are found in a classroom

chalk
students
blackboard
desks
teacher
books

Things you travel in

car
train
ship
airplane
taxi
bus

Things above you

sky
ceiling
moon
roof
stars
sun

Animals

deer
goat
bear
skunk
squirrel
tiger

Vegetables

squash
corn
tomato
beans
spinach
carrot

Clothing

- shirt
- pants
- socks
- underwear
- shoes
- hat

Parts of the body

- arm
- leg
- finger
- shoulder
- knee
- chest

Things you do with your feet

- walk
- kick
- jump
- dance
- run
- ski

Food

- spaghetti
- steak
- salad
- potato
- rice
- pizza

Stores

- hardware
- grocery
- drug
- music
- clothing
- shoe

Sports

- baseball
- basketball
- volleyball
- football
- soccer
- softball

Furniture

    sofa
    table
    armchair
    bed
    dresser
    coffee table

Relatives

    aunt
    brother
    cousin
    nephew
    grandmother
    father

Things you find in
a kitchen

    sink
    toaster
    napkins
    silverware
    refrigerator
    water

Things that you
listen to

    music
    radio
    teacher
    gossip
    tape recorder
    friend

Winter things

    snow
    Christmas
    skiing
    ice
    parka
    boots

Things that are
used by a child

    toy
    bicycle
    mittens
    kite
    shorts
    ball

Things to play

    soccer
    guitar
    games
    piano
    cards
    volleyball

Words that begin
with "f"

    friend
    flower
    fly
    France
    fat
    finger

Things that are
typically American

    hamburgers
    baseball
    hot dogs
    coca cola
    apple pie
    Empire State Building

Things that you
need to travel in
another country

    suitcase
    passport
    money
    ticket
    time
    dictionary

Things that are hot

    oven
    summer
    coffee
    Africa
    desert
    sun

Things that you
find at a university

    dormitory
    swimming pool
    cafeteria
    student union
    professors
    administration
      building

Things you find in Florida   Electrical appliances

    oranges   iron
    beach   hair dryer
    alligator   blender
    Miami   toaster
    sunshine   microwave oven
    palm trees   can opener

Things that are opened   Professions

    letter   teacher
    can   doctor
    gift   scientist
    door   lawyer
    box   accountant
    window   businessman

Two-word verbs   Things you find in
                                   a jewelry store

    call up   necklace
    hang up   watch
    look like   ring
    run into   bracelet
    do over   diamond
    get up   cuff links

Things that a carpenter needs/uses

> hammer
> nails
> saw
> toolbox
> tape measure
> wood

Things with a hole(s)

> doughnut
> record
> Swiss Cheese
> golf course
> pipe
> nose

Things that are large

> watermelon
> 747
> Alaska
> sky
> Pacific Ocean
> elephant

Words that end with "t"

> light
> sit
> elephant
> cat
> last
> fight

Things that are round

> plate
> doughnut
> zero
> basketball
> clock
> cookie

Things that are long and narrow

> spaghetti
> river
> sidewalk
> belt
> train
> Chile

Cocktail Party

BRIEF DESCRIPTION:

This is a role-playing exercise in which each participant receives a card describing a character whose identity he assumes. At the conclusion of the exercise the class identifies and describes the various people they have met in the exercise. The lives of the characters can be entwined or a plot can unfold to make the exercise more interesting.

PURPOSE:

The exercise requires the students to practice social conversation. It also requires them to listen carefully and at the conclusion of the exercise, remember and re-state what they have heard.

PREPARATION:

Write brief descriptions on the cards — one to a card. The game is best played by at least six and not more than 16 characters. In a game designed for a lower level, only a minimum of information (such as name, age, profession) need be given.

PROCEDURE:

1. Give the directions to the students. First, set the scene -- party, meeting, bus station, etc.

2. Tell the students they will assume the role of the character on their cards. Then give each student a card and ask them to study it.

3. Step out of the room and help students -- one at a time -- with questions about the information on their card.

4. Let the students mingle and talk to each other for 15 to 30 minutes.

5. When it seems that everybody has met everybody else, conclude the game.

6. Single out each character - one by one - and have the other students tell what they can remember about the character.

VARIATIONS:

1. At the end of the game, have the students write out the cast of characters, and then read their papers to each other and compare.

2. A position on a contemporary issue can be added to the information on each card so that the objective becomes to find out each character's opinion on the issue.

3. In a multi-lingual class, students can work in pairs. One student speaks his native language and his partner acts as an interpreter.

SUGGESTIONS:

1. Family gatherings*:

   family relationship/problems are discovered

2. Neighborhood party:

   the local gossip, entanglements, social concerns are learned.

3. School party:

   international students get together -- stereotypes, cultural problems arise.

4. Bus/Airplane trip*:

   passengers on a trip discover how their lives are entwined.

5. Business meeting:

   office politics and personal involvements come up.

6. Hollywood party:

   movie star relationships are uncovered -- can use names of actual stars.

7. Murder mystery*:

   group of people (family, hotel guests, etc.) discover a murder and decide who is the murderer.

8. Reunion:

   high school, college, foreign students, etc.

9. School/University Meeting:

   Student/classroom/administrative problems are discussed.

* See sample games on the following pages.

*Family Gathering**

1. Harold Pinton. 45 years old. Married. 3 children.
2. Virginia Pinton. 42 years old. Married to Harold Pinton.
3. Nancy Pinton. 21 years old. Father is Harold Pinton.
4. Jeff Pinton. 15 years old. Your mother is Barbara Pinton.
5. Barbara Pinton. 38 years old. Wife of Mark Pinton.
6. George Owens. 70 years old. You have one daughter who is married to Harold Pinton.
7. Mark Pinton. 40 years old. Son of John Pinton.
8. John Pinton. 75 years old. You have two sons — Harold and Mark.
9. Nora Pinton. 21 years old. You have a twin sister.
10. Steve Pinton. 18 years old. Your mother is Virginia Pinton. You have two sisters.
11. Alex Owens. 72 years old. Virginia Pinton is your niece.
12. Anne Owens. 42 years old. Harold is your brother-in-law.
13. Martha Pinton. 74 years old. Your grandson is Jeff.
14. Andy Pinton 17 years old. You are Harold Pinton's nephew.
15. Phyllis Pinton. 22 years old. Nora is your cousin.
16. Greg Pinton. 19 years old. You have two brothers.

*You do not need 16 people to play this game. The first eight characters are basic. Add others in sequence as you need them.

Murder Mystery

1.   Martin Danfield. You are 65 years old. You are wealthy and disliked by almost everyone. You are having a birthday party for your daughter, Leslie. After you finish your first drink, you die. Someone in the room has poisoned you.

2.   Sally Danfield. You are 35 years old. You married Martin Danfield two years ago. You married him for his money which you hope to get when he dies.

3.   Marsha Danfield. You are 62 years old. You had been married to Martin Danfield for 37 years when he asked you for a divorce in order to marry a younger woman. You and Martin have two children.

4.   Benjamin Danfield. You are 35 years old. You are the son of Martin and Marsha Danfield. Your father has recently fired you from his business, but you don't know why.

5.   Leslie Ellsworth. You are 32 years old. You are the daughter of Martin and Marsha Danfield. Your father, whom you love dearly has always given you everything you wanted and more. You are married to Dunton Ellsworth.

6.   Dunton Ellsworth. You are 38 years old. You are married to Leslie Ellsworth. You are the vice president of her father's business. You love to spend money, both yours and your wife's.

7.   Charles. You are the butler at the Danfield mansion. You are 65 years old. You have worked for the Danfield's for 37 years. You have never approved of Martin Danfield's divorce from Marsha and marriage to Sally. You dislike both Martin and Sally.

8. Rose. You are the wife of the butler, Charles. You have been the cook at the Danfield mansion for 37 years. You loved your work before Martin Danfield divorced his first wife, Marsha. You hate his new wife, Sally.

9. Carla Fleming. You are 32 years old. You are married to Chester Fleming, but you are really in love with Martin Danfield and his money.

10. Chester Fleming. You are Martin Danfield's best friend. You went to college together in the 1930's. You recently married your second wife who is thirty years younger than you. You have just poisoned Martin's drink because you discovered that he was seeing your new wife Carla, whom you love more than anything else in the world. Nobody knows you are the murderer.

Airplane Trip

1. Pedro Fernandez. You are 55 years old. You are a Mexican businessman who imports televisions from Europe. You are returning to Mexico after a business trip to New York. You wanted to begin importing American televisions, but you weren't successful in your meetings in New York.

2. Maria Fernandez. You are 45 years old. You are the wife of Pedro Fernandez. Ten years ago, a young American girl named Yvonne stayed in your house in Guadalajara, Mexico. You haven't seen her since then.

3. Yvonne Addley. You are 32 years old. You are married to Donald Addley. Ten years ago when you were single, you spent a summer in Mexico. You stayed with the family of Pedro Fernandez in Guadalajara. You are now going to Mexico on vacation and plan to visit your Mexican family and introduce them to your husband.

4. Donald Addley. You are 34 years old. You are
    married to Yvonne Addley. You and your wife
    are going to Mexico for a vacation.

5. Peggy Wallace. You are 23 years old and want to
    continue your study of medicine in Mexico. You
    are going to Mexico to have an interview at the
    University of Guadalajara.

6. Carlos Garcia. You are returning to Mexico from
    a trip to New York where you attended a medical
    convention. You are in charge of admissions at
    the medical college at the University of
    Guadalajara.

7. Toshihiro Sato. You own a Japanese television
    export business. You are going to Mexico because
    you would like to begin exporting your televisions
    to Mexico. You studied English and Spanish at
    the Tokyo Language Center in the 1950's.

8. Alice King. You are 55 years old. You are
    married to David King. Ten years ago you lived
    in Japan and taught English and Spanish at the
    Tokyo Language Center. One of your most
    memorable students was Toshihiro Sato.

9. David King. You and your wife, Alice, are going
    to Mexico for a vacation. You are the Dean of
    Admissions at the Northfield University Medical
    Center.

10. Ted Ward. You are 23 years old. You are one
    of the stewards on the flight to Mexico. Your
    high school girlfriend, whom you haven't seen for
    five years, is planning to study medicine in
    Mexico. Her name is Peggy Wallace.

Who's Who

BRIEF DESCRIPTION:

This is a variation of Twenty Questions. The number of questions is reduced to 10 and the field is reduced to categories of people, e.g. professions, or famous people. The class is divided into two teams and each team takes turns trying to guess the identities of the opposing players.

PURPOSE:

The game will require the students to practice yes-no questions. It can also serve as a vocabulary review of selected areas, e.g. music, sports, politics, etc.

PREPARATION:

Write the name of a famous person and (optionally) a brief descriptive phrase on each card. All the people should be in the same field, e.g. music. A sample card might read: Frank Sinatra, male vocalist; popular music; American.

PROCEDURE:

1. Describe the game to the students and tell what field the personalities are in. Emphasize that questions must be of the yes-no variety, and the respondent answers with only Yes or No. Explain that only 10 questions may be asked.

2. Divide the class into two teams and hand out the cards. Players may show their cards to others on their team.

3. Assist students who need help identifying their characters by stepping outside the room for private consultations.

4. Alternate the guessing from one team to the other until all students have been quizzed on the identity of their personalities.

5. The team with the most correct identifications wins.

VARIATIONS:

1. Set a time limit on each 10-question session. A 3-minute egg timer is useful for this.

2. Allow one or two Wh questions, except of course, "Who are you?"

3. If a team fails to guess the identity of the character, but can make a correct statement of five identifying facts, give them ½ point. Such a statement might be:

$$\overset{1}{\text{You}} \text{ are an } \overset{2}{\text{American}} \text{ singer} \overset{3}{\text{ of popular}}$$

$$\overset{4}{\text{music and you}} \text{ are } \overset{5}{\text{still living}}\ldots"$$

The statement must be grammatically correct as well as factually correct.

4. Give each student a blank card and announce the category. Each student writes a name he or she knows on his/her card. Walk around and check for duplicates. If two or more students have written the same name, you will probably want to have one of them change.

5. Put one student on the spot. Let everyone else know who the student is. The student must then ask the others questions to find out who he or she is.

64

SUGGESTIONS:

1. trades*, professions*, craftsmen

2. social roles (parent, friend, relative, etc.)

3. school positions (registrar, professor, librarian, coach, principal, etc.)

4. national leaders -- past* and present

5. heroes (contemporary, mythical, comic books)

6. artists and sculptors*

7. movie stars*

8. writers*

9. scientists*

10. philosophers

11. T.V. stars

12. local personalities

13. famous animals

14. athletes*

15. musicians*

* See sample games on the following pages.

Professions

doctor

scientist

lawyer

engineer

dentist

psychiatrist

airplane pilot

nurse

soldier

politician

accountant

artist

athlete

actor

writer

Trades

carpenter

plumber

electrician

bus driver

waiter

house painter

truck driver

elevator operator

sales clerk

janitor

taxi driver

mechanic

auto worker

miner

farmer

Political Leaders
(past)

Simón Bolívar — Venezuela

Mao Tse Tung — China

Winston Churchill — Britain

John F. Kennedy — United States

Julius Caesar — Rome (Italy)

Charles De Gaulle — France

Indira Gandhi — India

Elizabeth I — England

Jomo Kenyatta — Kenya

Kemal Atatürk — Turkey

Joseph Tito — Yugoslavia

Anwar Sadat — Egypt

Nikita Kruschev — Russia

Benito Juárez — Mexico

Haile Selassie — Ethiopia

Artists and Sculptors

John James Audubon - American wildlife artist

Benvenuto Cellini - Italian sculptor

Albrecht Dürer - German engraver

Leonardo da Vinci - Italian painter

Pablo Picasso - Spanish painter

Rembrandt - Dutch painter

Pierre-Auguste Renoir - French painter

Paul Gaugin - French painter

El Greco - Spanish painter

Mary Cassatt - American painter

Diego Rivera - Mexican muralist

Grandma Moses - American painter

Georgia O'Keefe - American painter

José Clemente Orozco - Mexican muralist

Movie Stars

Paul Newman

Charlie Chaplin

John Wayne

Sean Connery

Lawrence Olivier

Clark Gable

John Travolta

Marcello Mastroianni

Humphrey Bogart

Sophia Loren

Jane Fonda

Katherine Hepburn

Elizabeth Taylor

Marilyn Monroe

Brigitte Bardot

Glenda Jackson

Writers

H. G. Wells — British novelist

Leo Tolstoy — Russian novelist

Edgar Allen Poe — American poet,
                 short-story writer

Pablo Neruda — Chilean poet

Pearl Buck — American Novelist,
              short-story writer

Rudyard Kipling — British author, poet

Ernest Hemingway — American novelist,
                  short-story writer

Isak Dinesen — Danish author

Emily Dickinson — American poet

Jane Austen — British novelist

Agatha Christie — British mystery writer

Dante Alighieri — Italian poet

Anton Chekov — Russian dramatist,
              short-story writer

Omar Khayyam — Persian poet

Jules Verne — French novelist

Scientists

Marie Curie - Polish/French chemist

Charles Darwin - British naturalist

Thomas Edison - American inventor

Albert Einstein - American physicist

Enrico Fermi - Italian physicist

Sigmund Freud - Austrian psychiatrist

Galileo Galilei - Italian astronomer, physicist

Alexander Humboldt - German explorer, naturalist

Louis Pasteur - French chemist

Louis Leakey - British anthropologist

Rudolf Diesel - German mechanical engineer

Alexander Fleming - British bacteriologist

Isaac Newton - British mathematician, philosopher

Margaret Mead - American anthropologist

Carl Jung - Swiss psychiatrist

Athletes

Muhammad Ali — boxer; American

Magic Johnson — basketball player; American

Steffi Graf — tennis player; German

Nadia Comaneci — gymnast; Romanian

Pelé — soccer player; Brazilian

Joe Montana — football player; American

Sergei Bubka — pole vaulter; Russian

Yogi Berra — baseball player; American

Florence Griffith Joyner — runner; American

Alberto Tomba — skier; Italian

Chris Evert-Lloyd — tennis player; American

Bjorn Borg — tennis player; Swedish

Wayne Gretzky — hockey player; Canadian

Katarina Witt — figure skater; Germany

Martina Navratilova — tennis player;
                                    Czechoslovakian

Musicians

Frank Sinatra - popular and jazz singer; American

Olivia Newton-John - popular and rock singer; Australian

Seiji Ozawa - conductor, Boston Symphony Orchestra; Japanese

Andrés Segovia - classical guitarist; Spanish

Mick Jagger - rock singer; British

Ella Fitzgerald - jazz singer; American

Ludwig Beethoven - composer; German

Barbra Streisand - popular singer; American

Luciano Pavarotti - opera singer; Italian

Elvis Presley - rock singer; American

Joan Baez - folk singer; American

Heitor Villa-Lobos - composer; Brazilian

Linda Ronstadt - rock singer; American

John Lennon - rock singer and writer; British

Wolfgang Amadeus Mozart - composer, Austrian